I0062217

THIS BOOK BELONGS TO:

CONTACT INFORMATION	
NAME	
ADDRESS	
PHONE #	
EMAIL	

DEDICATION

This Order Log Book is dedicated to small business owners who want to keep accurate records and retain information for orders received.

You are my inspiration for producing this book and I'm honored to be a part of helping you manage and retain important information regarding your business.

HOW TO USE THIS BOOK

This Order Log Book will help you record, collect, and organize your information in an easy to use format.

Here are examples of information for you to fill in and write the details for your activities as a business owner.

Fill in the following information:

1. Order Form - record order number, date, customer name, address, phone number, and email

2. Order Status - checklist for an: order paid/method, shipped or canceled, record estimated shipping date, shipping company, shipping date, tracking number, and arrival date

3. Item Information - record item number, description, quantity, price, and the final price

4. Order Totals - record subtotal, discount, taxes, shipping, and grand total

5. Notes - space to write important details

ORDER FORM

ORDER #	
DATE	

CUSTOMER	
ADDRESS	
PHONE	
EMAIL	

STATUS	
O PAID / METHOD	
O SHIPPED	
O CANCELED	
EST. SHIPPING DATE	
SHIPPING COMPANY	
SHIPPING DATE	
TRACKING #	
ARRIVAL DATE	

ITEM #	DESCRIPTION	QTY	PRICE	FINAL PRICE

NOTES		SUBTOTAL	
		DISCOUNT	
		TAXES	
		SHIPPING	
		GRAND TOTAL	

ORDER FORM

ORDER #	
DATE	

CUSTOMER	
ADDRESS	
PHONE	
EMAIL	

STATUS	
O PAID / METHOD	
O SHIPPED	
O CANCELED	
EST. SHIPPING DATE	
SHIPPING COMPANY	
SHIPPING DATE	
TRACKING #	
ARRIVAL DATE	

ITEM #	DESCRIPTION	QTY	PRICE	FINAL PRICE

NOTES	SUBTOTAL	
	DISCOUNT	
	TAXES	
	SHIPPING	
	GRAND TOTAL	

ORDER FORM

ORDER #	
DATE	

CUSTOMER	
ADDRESS	
PHONE	
EMAIL	

STATUS

- O PAID / METHOD
- O SHIPPED
- O CANCELED

EST. SHIPPING DATE	
SHIPPING COMPANY	
SHIPPING DATE	
TRACKING #	
ARRIVAL DATE	

ITEM #	DESCRIPTION	QTY	PRICE	FINAL PRICE

NOTES	

SUBTOTAL	
DISCOUNT	
TAXES	
SHIPPING	
GRAND TOTAL	

ORDER FORM

ORDER #	
DATE	

CUSTOMER	
ADDRESS	
PHONE	
EMAIL	

STATUS	
O PAID / METHOD	
O SHIPPED	
O CANCELED	
EST. SHIPPING DATE	
SHIPPING COMPANY	
SHIPPING DATE	
TRACKING #	
ARRIVAL DATE	

ITEM #	DESCRIPTION	QTY	PRICE	FINAL PRICE

NOTES

SUBTOTAL	
DISCOUNT	
TAXES	
SHIPPING	
GRAND TOTAL	

ORDER FORM

ORDER #	
DATE	

CUSTOMER	
ADDRESS	
PHONE	
EMAIL	

STATUS	
O PAID / METHOD	
O SHIPPED	
O CANCELED	
EST. SHIPPING DATE	
SHIPPING COMPANY	
SHIPPING DATE	
TRACKING #	
ARRIVAL DATE	

ITEM #	DESCRIPTION	QTY	PRICE	FINAL PRICE

NOTES		SUBTOTAL	
		DISCOUNT	
		TAXES	
		SHIPPING	
		GRAND TOTAL	

ORDER FORM

ORDER #	
DATE	

CUSTOMER	
ADDRESS	
PHONE	
EMAIL	

STATUS	
O PAID / METHOD	
O SHIPPED	
O CANCELED	
EST. SHIPPING DATE	
SHIPPING COMPANY	
SHIPPING DATE	
TRACKING #	
ARRIVAL DATE	

ITEM #	DESCRIPTION	QTY	PRICE	FINAL PRICE

NOTES

SUBTOTAL	
DISCOUNT	
TAXES	
SHIPPING	
GRAND TOTAL	

ORDER FORM

ORDER #	
DATE	

CUSTOMER	
ADDRESS	
PHONE	
EMAIL	

STATUS	
O PAID / METHOD	
O SHIPPED	
O CANCELED	
EST. SHIPPING DATE	
SHIPPING COMPANY	
SHIPPING DATE	
TRACKING #	
ARRIVAL DATE	

ITEM #	DESCRIPTION	QTY	PRICE	FINAL PRICE

NOTES	SUBTOTAL	
	DISCOUNT	
	TAXES	
	SHIPPING	
	GRAND TOTAL	

ORDER FORM

ORDER #	
DATE	

CUSTOMER	
ADDRESS	
PHONE	
EMAIL	

STATUS	
O PAID / METHOD	
O SHIPPED	
O CANCELED	
EST. SHIPPING DATE	
SHIPPING COMPANY	
SHIPPING DATE	
TRACKING #	
ARRIVAL DATE	

ITEM #	DESCRIPTION	QTY	PRICE	FINAL PRICE

NOTES

SUBTOTAL	
DISCOUNT	
TAXES	
SHIPPING	
GRAND TOTAL	

ORDER FORM

ORDER #	
DATE	

CUSTOMER	
ADDRESS	
PHONE	
EMAIL	

STATUS	
O PAID / METHOD	
O SHIPPED	
O CANCELED	
EST. SHIPPING DATE	
SHIPPING COMPANY	
SHIPPING DATE	
TRACKING #	
ARRIVAL DATE	

ITEM #	DESCRIPTION	QTY	PRICE	FINAL PRICE

NOTES

SUBTOTAL	
DISCOUNT	
TAXES	
SHIPPING	
GRAND TOTAL	

ORDER FORM

ORDER #	
DATE	

CUSTOMER	
ADDRESS	
PHONE	
EMAIL	

STATUS	
O PAID / METHOD	
O SHIPPED	
O CANCELED	
EST. SHIPPING DATE	
SHIPPING COMPANY	
SHIPPING DATE	
TRACKING #	
ARRIVAL DATE	

ITEM #	DESCRIPTION	QTY	PRICE	FINAL PRICE

NOTES		SUBTOTAL	
		DISCOUNT	
		TAXES	
		SHIPPING	
		GRAND TOTAL	

ORDER FORM

ORDER #	
DATE	

CUSTOMER	
ADDRESS	
PHONE	
EMAIL	

STATUS

O PAID / METHOD

O SHIPPED

O CANCELED

EST. SHIPPING DATE	
SHIPPING COMPANY	
SHIPPING DATE	
TRACKING #	
ARRIVAL DATE	

ITEM #	DESCRIPTION	QTY	PRICE	FINAL PRICE

NOTES	SUBTOTAL	
	DISCOUNT	
	TAXES	
	SHIPPING	
	GRAND TOTAL	

ORDER FORM

ORDER #	
DATE	

CUSTOMER	
ADDRESS	
PHONE	
EMAIL	

STATUS	
O PAID / METHOD	
O SHIPPED	
O CANCELED	
EST. SHIPPING DATE	
SHIPPING COMPANY	
SHIPPING DATE	
TRACKING #	
ARRIVAL DATE	

ITEM #	DESCRIPTION	QTY	PRICE	FINAL PRICE

NOTES		SUBTOTAL	
		DISCOUNT	
		TAXES	
		SHIPPING	
		GRAND TOTAL	

ORDER FORM

ORDER #	
DATE	

CUSTOMER	
ADDRESS	
PHONE	
EMAIL	

STATUS	
O PAID / METHOD	
O SHIPPED	
O CANCELED	
EST. SHIPPING DATE	
SHIPPING COMPANY	
SHIPPING DATE	
TRACKING #	
ARRIVAL DATE	

ITEM #	DESCRIPTION	QTY	PRICE	FINAL PRICE

NOTES

SUBTOTAL	
DISCOUNT	
TAXES	
SHIPPING	
GRAND TOTAL	

ORDER FORM

ORDER #	
DATE	

CUSTOMER	
ADDRESS	
PHONE	
EMAIL	

STATUS	
O PAID / METHOD	
O SHIPPED	
O CANCELED	
EST. SHIPPING DATE	
SHIPPING COMPANY	
SHIPPING DATE	
TRACKING #	
ARRIVAL DATE	

ITEM #	DESCRIPTION	QTY	PRICE	FINAL PRICE

NOTES	SUBTOTAL	
	DISCOUNT	
	TAXES	
	SHIPPING	
	GRAND TOTAL	

ORDER FORM

ORDER #	
DATE	

CUSTOMER	
ADDRESS	
PHONE	
EMAIL	

STATUS	
O PAID / METHOD	
O SHIPPED	
O CANCELED	
EST. SHIPPING DATE	
SHIPPING COMPANY	
SHIPPING DATE	
TRACKING #	
ARRIVAL DATE	

ITEM #	DESCRIPTION	QTY	PRICE	FINAL PRICE

NOTES

SUBTOTAL	
DISCOUNT	
TAXES	
SHIPPING	
GRAND TOTAL	

ORDER FORM

ORDER #	
DATE	

CUSTOMER	
ADDRESS	
PHONE	
EMAIL	

STATUS	
O PAID / METHOD	
O SHIPPED	
O CANCELED	
EST. SHIPPING DATE	
SHIPPING COMPANY	
SHIPPING DATE	
TRACKING #	
ARRIVAL DATE	

ITEM #	DESCRIPTION	QTY	PRICE	FINAL PRICE

NOTES	SUBTOTAL	
	DISCOUNT	
	TAXES	
	SHIPPING	
	GRAND TOTAL	

ORDER FORM

ORDER #	
DATE	

CUSTOMER	
ADDRESS	
PHONE	
EMAIL	

STATUS	
O PAID / METHOD	
O SHIPPED	
O CANCELED	
EST. SHIPPING DATE	
SHIPPING COMPANY	
SHIPPING DATE	
TRACKING #	
ARRIVAL DATE	

ITEM #	DESCRIPTION	QTY	PRICE	FINAL PRICE

NOTES		SUBTOTAL	
		DISCOUNT	
		TAXES	
		SHIPPING	
		GRAND TOTAL	

ORDER FORM

ORDER #	
DATE	

CUSTOMER	
ADDRESS	
PHONE	
EMAIL	

STATUS	
O PAID / METHOD	
O SHIPPED	
O CANCELED	
EST. SHIPPING DATE	
SHIPPING COMPANY	
SHIPPING DATE	
TRACKING #	
ARRIVAL DATE	

ITEM #	DESCRIPTION	QTY	PRICE	FINAL PRICE

NOTES		SUBTOTAL	
		DISCOUNT	
		TAXES	
		SHIPPING	
		GRAND TOTAL	

ORDER FORM

ORDER #	
DATE	

CUSTOMER	
ADDRESS	
PHONE	
EMAIL	

STATUS	
O PAID / METHOD	
O SHIPPED	
O CANCELED	
EST. SHIPPING DATE	
SHIPPING COMPANY	
SHIPPING DATE	
TRACKING #	
ARRIVAL DATE	

ITEM #	DESCRIPTION	QTY	PRICE	FINAL PRICE

NOTES		SUBTOTAL	
		DISCOUNT	
		TAXES	
		SHIPPING	
		GRAND TOTAL	

ORDER FORM

ORDER #	
DATE	

CUSTOMER	
ADDRESS	
PHONE	
EMAIL	

STATUS	
O PAID / METHOD	
O SHIPPED	
O CANCELED	
EST. SHIPPING DATE	
SHIPPING COMPANY	
SHIPPING DATE	
TRACKING #	
ARRIVAL DATE	

ITEM #	DESCRIPTION	QTY	PRICE	FINAL PRICE

NOTES

SUBTOTAL	
DISCOUNT	
TAXES	
SHIPPING	
GRAND TOTAL	

ORDER FORM

ORDER #	
DATE	

CUSTOMER	
ADDRESS	
PHONE	
EMAIL	

STATUS	
O PAID / METHOD	
O SHIPPED	
O CANCELED	
EST. SHIPPING DATE	
SHIPPING COMPANY	
SHIPPING DATE	
TRACKING #	
ARRIVAL DATE	

ITEM #	DESCRIPTION	QTY	PRICE	FINAL PRICE

NOTES		SUBTOTAL	
		DISCOUNT	
		TAXES	
		SHIPPING	
		GRAND TOTAL	

ORDER FORM

ORDER #	
DATE	

STATUS	
O PAID / METHOD	
O SHIPPED	
O CANCELED	

CUSTOMER	
ADDRESS	
PHONE	
EMAIL	

EST. SHIPPING DATE	
SHIPPING COMPANY	
SHIPPING DATE	
TRACKING #	
ARRIVAL DATE	

ITEM #	DESCRIPTION	QTY	PRICE	FINAL PRICE

NOTES

SUBTOTAL	
DISCOUNT	
TAXES	
SHIPPING	
GRAND TOTAL	

ORDER FORM

ORDER #	
DATE	

CUSTOMER	
ADDRESS	
PHONE	
EMAIL	

STATUS	
O PAID / METHOD	
O SHIPPED	
O CANCELED	
EST. SHIPPING DATE	
SHIPPING COMPANY	
SHIPPING DATE	
TRACKING #	
ARRIVAL DATE	

ITEM #	DESCRIPTION	QTY	PRICE	FINAL PRICE

NOTES		SUBTOTAL	
		DISCOUNT	
		TAXES	
		SHIPPING	
		GRAND TOTAL	

ORDER FORM

ORDER #	
DATE	

CUSTOMER	
ADDRESS	
PHONE	
EMAIL	

STATUS	
O PAID / METHOD	
O SHIPPED	
O CANCELED	
EST. SHIPPING DATE	
SHIPPING COMPANY	
SHIPPING DATE	
TRACKING #	
ARRIVAL DATE	

ITEM #	DESCRIPTION	QTY	PRICE	FINAL PRICE

NOTES	SUBTOTAL	
	DISCOUNT	
	TAXES	
	SHIPPING	
	GRAND TOTAL	

ORDER FORM

ORDER #	
DATE	

CUSTOMER	
ADDRESS	
PHONE	
EMAIL	

STATUS	
O PAID / METHOD	
O SHIPPED	
O CANCELED	
EST. SHIPPING DATE	
SHIPPING COMPANY	
SHIPPING DATE	
TRACKING #	
ARRIVAL DATE	

ITEM #	DESCRIPTION	QTY	PRICE	FINAL PRICE

NOTES

SUBTOTAL	
DISCOUNT	
TAXES	
SHIPPING	
GRAND TOTAL	

ORDER FORM

ORDER #	
DATE	

CUSTOMER	
ADDRESS	
PHONE	
EMAIL	

STATUS	
O PAID / METHOD	
O SHIPPED	
O CANCELED	
EST. SHIPPING DATE	
SHIPPING COMPANY	
SHIPPING DATE	
TRACKING #	
ARRIVAL DATE	

ITEM #	DESCRIPTION	QTY	PRICE	FINAL PRICE

NOTES	SUBTOTAL	
	DISCOUNT	
	TAXES	
	SHIPPING	
	GRAND TOTAL	

ORDER FORM

ORDER #	
DATE	

CUSTOMER	
ADDRESS	
PHONE	
EMAIL	

STATUS	
O PAID / METHOD	
O SHIPPED	
O CANCELED	
EST. SHIPPING DATE	
SHIPPING COMPANY	
SHIPPING DATE	
TRACKING #	
ARRIVAL DATE	

ITEM #	DESCRIPTION	QTY	PRICE	FINAL PRICE

NOTES	SUBTOTAL	
	DISCOUNT	
	TAXES	
	SHIPPING	
	GRAND TOTAL	

ORDER FORM

ORDER #	
DATE	

CUSTOMER	
ADDRESS	
PHONE	
EMAIL	

STATUS	
O PAID / METHOD	
O SHIPPED	
O CANCELED	
EST. SHIPPING DATE	
SHIPPING COMPANY	
SHIPPING DATE	
TRACKING #	
ARRIVAL DATE	

ITEM #	DESCRIPTION	QTY	PRICE	FINAL PRICE

NOTES

SUBTOTAL	
DISCOUNT	
TAXES	
SHIPPING	
GRAND TOTAL	

ORDER FORM

ORDER #	
DATE	

CUSTOMER	
ADDRESS	
PHONE	
EMAIL	

STATUS	
O PAID / METHOD	
O SHIPPED	
O CANCELED	
EST. SHIPPING DATE	
SHIPPING COMPANY	
SHIPPING DATE	
TRACKING #	
ARRIVAL DATE	

ITEM #	DESCRIPTION	QTY	PRICE	FINAL PRICE

NOTES		SUBTOTAL	
		DISCOUNT	
		TAXES	
		SHIPPING	
		GRAND TOTAL	

ORDER FORM

ORDER #	
DATE	

CUSTOMER	
ADDRESS	
PHONE	
EMAIL	

STATUS	
O PAID / METHOD	
O SHIPPED	
O CANCELED	
EST. SHIPPING DATE	
SHIPPING COMPANY	
SHIPPING DATE	
TRACKING #	
ARRIVAL DATE	

ITEM #	DESCRIPTION	QTY	PRICE	FINAL PRICE

NOTES

SUBTOTAL	
DISCOUNT	
TAXES	
SHIPPING	
GRAND TOTAL	

ORDER FORM

ORDER #	
DATE	

CUSTOMER	
ADDRESS	
PHONE	
EMAIL	

STATUS

O PAID / METHOD

O SHIPPED

O CANCELED

EST. SHIPPING DATE	
SHIPPING COMPANY	
SHIPPING DATE	
TRACKING #	
ARRIVAL DATE	

ITEM #	DESCRIPTION	QTY	PRICE	FINAL PRICE

NOTES

SUBTOTAL	
DISCOUNT	
TAXES	
SHIPPING	
GRAND TOTAL	

ORDER FORM

ORDER #	
DATE	

CUSTOMER	
ADDRESS	
PHONE	
EMAIL	

STATUS	
O PAID / METHOD	
O SHIPPED	
O CANCELED	
EST. SHIPPING DATE	
SHIPPING COMPANY	
SHIPPING DATE	
TRACKING #	
ARRIVAL DATE	

ITEM #	DESCRIPTION	QTY	PRICE	FINAL PRICE

NOTES		SUBTOTAL	
		DISCOUNT	
		TAXES	
		SHIPPING	
		GRAND TOTAL	

ORDER FORM

ORDER #	
DATE	

CUSTOMER	
ADDRESS	
PHONE	
EMAIL	

STATUS	
O PAID / METHOD	
O SHIPPED	
O CANCELED	
EST. SHIPPING DATE	
SHIPPING COMPANY	
SHIPPING DATE	
TRACKING #	
ARRIVAL DATE	

ITEM #	DESCRIPTION	QTY	PRICE	FINAL PRICE

NOTES

SUBTOTAL	
DISCOUNT	
TAXES	
SHIPPING	
GRAND TOTAL	

ORDER FORM

ORDER #	
DATE	

CUSTOMER	
ADDRESS	
PHONE	
EMAIL	

STATUS	
O PAID / METHOD	
O SHIPPED	
O CANCELED	
EST. SHIPPING DATE	
SHIPPING COMPANY	
SHIPPING DATE	
TRACKING #	
ARRIVAL DATE	

ITEM #	DESCRIPTION	QTY	PRICE	FINAL PRICE

NOTES	SUBTOTAL	
	DISCOUNT	
	TAXES	
	SHIPPING	
	GRAND TOTAL	

ORDER FORM

ORDER #	
DATE	

CUSTOMER	
ADDRESS	
PHONE	
EMAIL	

STATUS	
O PAID / METHOD	
O SHIPPED	
O CANCELED	
EST. SHIPPING DATE	
SHIPPING COMPANY	
SHIPPING DATE	
TRACKING #	
ARRIVAL DATE	

ITEM #	DESCRIPTION	QTY	PRICE	FINAL PRICE

NOTES	SUBTOTAL	
	DISCOUNT	
	TAXES	
	SHIPPING	
	GRAND TOTAL	

ORDER FORM

ORDER #	
DATE	

CUSTOMER	
ADDRESS	
PHONE	
EMAIL	

STATUS	
O PAID / METHOD	
O SHIPPED	
O CANCELED	
EST. SHIPPING DATE	
SHIPPING COMPANY	
SHIPPING DATE	
TRACKING #	
ARRIVAL DATE	

ITEM #	DESCRIPTION	QTY	PRICE	FINAL PRICE

NOTES	SUBTOTAL	
	DISCOUNT	
	TAXES	
	SHIPPING	
	GRAND TOTAL	

ORDER FORM

ORDER #	
DATE	

CUSTOMER	
ADDRESS	
PHONE	
EMAIL	

STATUS	
O PAID / METHOD	
O SHIPPED	
O CANCELED	
EST. SHIPPING DATE	
SHIPPING COMPANY	
SHIPPING DATE	
TRACKING #	
ARRIVAL DATE	

ITEM #	DESCRIPTION	QTY	PRICE	FINAL PRICE

NOTES		SUBTOTAL	
		DISCOUNT	
		TAXES	
		SHIPPING	
		GRAND TOTAL	

ORDER FORM

ORDER #	
DATE	

CUSTOMER	
ADDRESS	
PHONE	
EMAIL	

STATUS	
O PAID / METHOD	
O SHIPPED	
O CANCELED	
EST. SHIPPING DATE	
SHIPPING COMPANY	
SHIPPING DATE	
TRACKING #	
ARRIVAL DATE	

ITEM #	DESCRIPTION	QTY	PRICE	FINAL PRICE

NOTES	SUBTOTAL	
	DISCOUNT	
	TAXES	
	SHIPPING	
	GRAND TOTAL	

ORDER FORM

ORDER #	
DATE	

CUSTOMER	
ADDRESS	
PHONE	
EMAIL	

STATUS	
O PAID / METHOD	
O SHIPPED	
O CANCELED	
EST. SHIPPING DATE	
SHIPPING COMPANY	
SHIPPING DATE	
TRACKING #	
ARRIVAL DATE	

ITEM #	DESCRIPTION	QTY	PRICE	FINAL PRICE

NOTES

SUBTOTAL	
DISCOUNT	
TAXES	
SHIPPING	
GRAND TOTAL	

ORDER FORM

ORDER #	
DATE	

STATUS	
O PAID / METHOD	
O SHIPPED	
O CANCELED	

CUSTOMER	
ADDRESS	
PHONE	
EMAIL	

EST. SHIPPING DATE	
SHIPPING COMPANY	
SHIPPING DATE	
TRACKING #	
ARRIVAL DATE	

ITEM #	DESCRIPTION	QTY	PRICE	FINAL PRICE

NOTES

SUBTOTAL	
DISCOUNT	
TAXES	
SHIPPING	
GRAND TOTAL	

ORDER FORM

ORDER #	
DATE	

CUSTOMER	
ADDRESS	
PHONE	
EMAIL	

STATUS	
O PAID / METHOD	
O SHIPPED	
O CANCELED	
EST. SHIPPING DATE	
SHIPPING COMPANY	
SHIPPING DATE	
TRACKING #	
ARRIVAL DATE	

ITEM #	DESCRIPTION	QTY	PRICE	FINAL PRICE

NOTES

SUBTOTAL	
DISCOUNT	
TAXES	
SHIPPING	
GRAND TOTAL	

ORDER FORM

ORDER #	
DATE	

CUSTOMER	
ADDRESS	
PHONE	
EMAIL	

STATUS	
O PAID / METHOD	
O SHIPPED	
O CANCELED	
EST. SHIPPING DATE	
SHIPPING COMPANY	
SHIPPING DATE	
TRACKING #	
ARRIVAL DATE	

ITEM #	DESCRIPTION	QTY	PRICE	FINAL PRICE

NOTES	SUBTOTAL	
	DISCOUNT	
	TAXES	
	SHIPPING	
	GRAND TOTAL	

ORDER FORM

ORDER #	
DATE	

CUSTOMER	
ADDRESS	
PHONE	
EMAIL	

STATUS	
O PAID / METHOD	
O SHIPPED	
O CANCELED	
EST. SHIPPING DATE	
SHIPPING COMPANY	
SHIPPING DATE	
TRACKING #	
ARRIVAL DATE	

ITEM #	DESCRIPTION	QTY	PRICE	FINAL PRICE

NOTES		SUBTOTAL	
		DISCOUNT	
		TAXES	
		SHIPPING	
		GRAND TOTAL	

ORDER FORM

ORDER #	
DATE	

CUSTOMER	
ADDRESS	
PHONE	
EMAIL	

STATUS

O PAID / METHOD

O SHIPPED

O CANCELED

EST. SHIPPING DATE	
SHIPPING COMPANY	
SHIPPING DATE	
TRACKING #	
ARRIVAL DATE	

ITEM #	DESCRIPTION	QTY	PRICE	FINAL PRICE

NOTES	SUBTOTAL	
	DISCOUNT	
	TAXES	
	SHIPPING	
	GRAND TOTAL	

ORDER FORM

ORDER #	
DATE	

CUSTOMER	
ADDRESS	
PHONE	
EMAIL	

STATUS	
O PAID / METHOD	
O SHIPPED	
O CANCELED	
EST. SHIPPING DATE	
SHIPPING COMPANY	
SHIPPING DATE	
TRACKING #	
ARRIVAL DATE	

ITEM #	DESCRIPTION	QTY	PRICE	FINAL PRICE

NOTES	SUBTOTAL	
	DISCOUNT	
	TAXES	
	SHIPPING	
	GRAND TOTAL	

ORDER FORM

ORDER #	
DATE	

CUSTOMER	
ADDRESS	
PHONE	
EMAIL	

STATUS	
O PAID / METHOD	
O SHIPPED	
O CANCELED	
EST. SHIPPING DATE	
SHIPPING COMPANY	
SHIPPING DATE	
TRACKING #	
ARRIVAL DATE	

ITEM #	DESCRIPTION	QTY	PRICE	FINAL PRICE

NOTES

SUBTOTAL	
DISCOUNT	
TAXES	
SHIPPING	
GRAND TOTAL	

ORDER FORM

ORDER #	
DATE	

CUSTOMER	
ADDRESS	
PHONE	
EMAIL	

STATUS	
O PAID / METHOD	
O SHIPPED	
O CANCELED	
EST. SHIPPING DATE	
SHIPPING COMPANY	
SHIPPING DATE	
TRACKING #	
ARRIVAL DATE	

ITEM #	DESCRIPTION	QTY	PRICE	FINAL PRICE

NOTES

SUBTOTAL	
DISCOUNT	
TAXES	
SHIPPING	
GRAND TOTAL	

ORDER FORM

ORDER #	
DATE	

CUSTOMER	
ADDRESS	
PHONE	
EMAIL	

STATUS	
O PAID / METHOD	
O SHIPPED	
O CANCELED	
EST. SHIPPING DATE	
SHIPPING COMPANY	
SHIPPING DATE	
TRACKING #	
ARRIVAL DATE	

ITEM #	DESCRIPTION	QTY	PRICE	FINAL PRICE

NOTES

SUBTOTAL	
DISCOUNT	
TAXES	
SHIPPING	
GRAND TOTAL	

ORDER FORM

ORDER #	
DATE	

CUSTOMER	
ADDRESS	
PHONE	
EMAIL	

STATUS	
O PAID / METHOD	
O SHIPPED	
O CANCELED	
EST. SHIPPING DATE	
SHIPPING COMPANY	
SHIPPING DATE	
TRACKING #	
ARRIVAL DATE	

ITEM #	DESCRIPTION	QTY	PRICE	FINAL PRICE

NOTES	SUBTOTAL	
	DISCOUNT	
	TAXES	
	SHIPPING	
	GRAND TOTAL	

ORDER FORM

ORDER #	
DATE	

CUSTOMER	
ADDRESS	
PHONE	
EMAIL	

STATUS	
O PAID / METHOD	
O SHIPPED	
O CANCELED	
EST. SHIPPING DATE	
SHIPPING COMPANY	
SHIPPING DATE	
TRACKING #	
ARRIVAL DATE	

ITEM #	DESCRIPTION	QTY	PRICE	FINAL PRICE

NOTES

SUBTOTAL	
DISCOUNT	
TAXES	
SHIPPING	
GRAND TOTAL	

ORDER FORM

ORDER #	
DATE	

CUSTOMER	
ADDRESS	
PHONE	
EMAIL	

STATUS	
O PAID / METHOD	
O SHIPPED	
O CANCELED	
EST. SHIPPING DATE	
SHIPPING COMPANY	
SHIPPING DATE	
TRACKING #	
ARRIVAL DATE	

ITEM #	DESCRIPTION	QTY	PRICE	FINAL PRICE

NOTES		SUBTOTAL	
		DISCOUNT	
		TAXES	
		SHIPPING	
		GRAND TOTAL	

ORDER FORM

ORDER #	
DATE	

CUSTOMER	
ADDRESS	
PHONE	
EMAIL	

STATUS	
O PAID / METHOD	
O SHIPPED	
O CANCELED	
EST. SHIPPING DATE	
SHIPPING COMPANY	
SHIPPING DATE	
TRACKING #	
ARRIVAL DATE	

ITEM #	DESCRIPTION	QTY	PRICE	FINAL PRICE

NOTES	SUBTOTAL	
	DISCOUNT	
	TAXES	
	SHIPPING	
	GRAND TOTAL	

ORDER FORM

ORDER #	
DATE	

CUSTOMER	
ADDRESS	
PHONE	
EMAIL	

STATUS	
O PAID / METHOD	
O SHIPPED	
O CANCELED	
EST. SHIPPING DATE	
SHIPPING COMPANY	
SHIPPING DATE	
TRACKING #	
ARRIVAL DATE	

ITEM #	DESCRIPTION	QTY	PRICE	FINAL PRICE

NOTES	SUBTOTAL	
	DISCOUNT	
	TAXES	
	SHIPPING	
	GRAND TOTAL	

ORDER FORM

ORDER #	
DATE	

STATUS	
O PAID / METHOD	
O SHIPPED	
O CANCELED	

CUSTOMER	

ADDRESS	

PHONE	
EMAIL	

EST. SHIPPING DATE	
SHIPPING COMPANY	
SHIPPING DATE	
TRACKING #	
ARRIVAL DATE	

ITEM #	DESCRIPTION	QTY	PRICE	FINAL PRICE

NOTES

SUBTOTAL	
DISCOUNT	
TAXES	
SHIPPING	
GRAND TOTAL	

ORDER FORM

ORDER #	
DATE	

CUSTOMER	
ADDRESS	
PHONE	
EMAIL	

STATUS	
O PAID / METHOD	
O SHIPPED	
O CANCELED	
EST. SHIPPING DATE	
SHIPPING COMPANY	
SHIPPING DATE	
TRACKING #	
ARRIVAL DATE	

ITEM #	DESCRIPTION	QTY	PRICE	FINAL PRICE

NOTES		SUBTOTAL	
		DISCOUNT	
		TAXES	
		SHIPPING	
		GRAND TOTAL	

ORDER FORM

ORDER #	
DATE	

CUSTOMER	
ADDRESS	
PHONE	
EMAIL	

STATUS	
O PAID / METHOD	
O SHIPPED	
O CANCELED	
EST. SHIPPING DATE	
SHIPPING COMPANY	
SHIPPING DATE	
TRACKING #	
ARRIVAL DATE	

ITEM #	DESCRIPTION	QTY	PRICE	FINAL PRICE

NOTES		SUBTOTAL	
		DISCOUNT	
		TAXES	
		SHIPPING	
		GRAND TOTAL	

ORDER FORM

ORDER #	
DATE	

CUSTOMER	
ADDRESS	
PHONE	
EMAIL	

STATUS	
O PAID / METHOD	
O SHIPPED	
O CANCELED	
EST. SHIPPING DATE	
SHIPPING COMPANY	
SHIPPING DATE	
TRACKING #	
ARRIVAL DATE	

ITEM #	DESCRIPTION	QTY	PRICE	FINAL PRICE

NOTES

SUBTOTAL	
DISCOUNT	
TAXES	
SHIPPING	
GRAND TOTAL	

ORDER FORM

ORDER #	
DATE	

CUSTOMER	
ADDRESS	
PHONE	
EMAIL	

STATUS

O PAID / METHOD

O SHIPPED

O CANCELED

EST. SHIPPING DATE	
SHIPPING COMPANY	
SHIPPING DATE	
TRACKING #	
ARRIVAL DATE	

ITEM #	DESCRIPTION	QTY	PRICE	FINAL PRICE

NOTES

SUBTOTAL	
DISCOUNT	
TAXES	
SHIPPING	
GRAND TOTAL	

ORDER FORM

ORDER #	
DATE	

CUSTOMER	
ADDRESS	
PHONE	
EMAIL	

STATUS	
O PAID / METHOD	
O SHIPPED	
O CANCELED	
EST. SHIPPING DATE	
SHIPPING COMPANY	
SHIPPING DATE	
TRACKING #	
ARRIVAL DATE	

ITEM #	DESCRIPTION	QTY	PRICE	FINAL PRICE

NOTES	
	SUBTOTAL	
	DISCOUNT	
	TAXES	
	SHIPPING	
	GRAND TOTAL	

ORDER FORM

ORDER #	
DATE	

STATUS	
O PAID / METHOD	
O SHIPPED	
O CANCELED	

CUSTOMER	
ADDRESS	
PHONE	
EMAIL	

EST. SHIPPING DATE	
SHIPPING COMPANY	
SHIPPING DATE	
TRACKING #	
ARRIVAL DATE	

ITEM #	DESCRIPTION	QTY	PRICE	FINAL PRICE

NOTES

SUBTOTAL	
DISCOUNT	
TAXES	
SHIPPING	
GRAND TOTAL	

ORDER FORM

ORDER #	
DATE	

CUSTOMER	
ADDRESS	
PHONE	
EMAIL	

STATUS	
O PAID / METHOD	
O SHIPPED	
O CANCELED	
EST. SHIPPING DATE	
SHIPPING COMPANY	
SHIPPING DATE	
TRACKING #	
ARRIVAL DATE	

ITEM #	DESCRIPTION	QTY	PRICE	FINAL PRICE

NOTES	SUBTOTAL	
	DISCOUNT	
	TAXES	
	SHIPPING	
	GRAND TOTAL	

ORDER FORM

ORDER #	
DATE	

CUSTOMER	
ADDRESS	
PHONE	
EMAIL	

STATUS	
O PAID / METHOD	
O SHIPPED	
O CANCELED	
EST. SHIPPING DATE	
SHIPPING COMPANY	
SHIPPING DATE	
TRACKING #	
ARRIVAL DATE	

ITEM #	DESCRIPTION	QTY	PRICE	FINAL PRICE

NOTES	SUBTOTAL	
	DISCOUNT	
	TAXES	
	SHIPPING	
	GRAND TOTAL	

ORDER FORM

ORDER #	
DATE	

CUSTOMER	
ADDRESS	
PHONE	
EMAIL	

STATUS	
O PAID / METHOD	
O SHIPPED	
O CANCELED	
EST. SHIPPING DATE	
SHIPPING COMPANY	
SHIPPING DATE	
TRACKING #	
ARRIVAL DATE	

ITEM #	DESCRIPTION	QTY	PRICE	FINAL PRICE

NOTES

SUBTOTAL	
DISCOUNT	
TAXES	
SHIPPING	
GRAND TOTAL	

ORDER FORM

ORDER #	
DATE	

CUSTOMER	
ADDRESS	
PHONE	
EMAIL	

STATUS

O PAID / METHOD

O SHIPPED

O CANCELED

EST. SHIPPING DATE	
SHIPPING COMPANY	
SHIPPING DATE	
TRACKING #	
ARRIVAL DATE	

ITEM #	DESCRIPTION	QTY	PRICE	FINAL PRICE

NOTES		SUBTOTAL	
		DISCOUNT	
		TAXES	
		SHIPPING	
		GRAND TOTAL	

ORDER FORM

ORDER #	
DATE	

CUSTOMER	
ADDRESS	
PHONE	
EMAIL	

STATUS	
O PAID / METHOD	
O SHIPPED	
O CANCELED	
EST. SHIPPING DATE	
SHIPPING COMPANY	
SHIPPING DATE	
TRACKING #	
ARRIVAL DATE	

ITEM #	DESCRIPTION	QTY	PRICE	FINAL PRICE

NOTES	SUBTOTAL	
	DISCOUNT	
	TAXES	
	SHIPPING	
	GRAND TOTAL	

ORDER FORM

ORDER #	
DATE	

CUSTOMER	
ADDRESS	
PHONE	
EMAIL	

STATUS	
O PAID / METHOD	
O SHIPPED	
O CANCELED	
EST. SHIPPING DATE	
SHIPPING COMPANY	
SHIPPING DATE	
TRACKING #	
ARRIVAL DATE	

ITEM #	DESCRIPTION	QTY	PRICE	FINAL PRICE

NOTES		SUBTOTAL	
		DISCOUNT	
		TAXES	
		SHIPPING	
		GRAND TOTAL	

ORDER FORM

ORDER #	
DATE	

CUSTOMER	
ADDRESS	
PHONE	
EMAIL	

STATUS	
O PAID / METHOD	
O SHIPPED	
O CANCELED	
EST. SHIPPING DATE	
SHIPPING COMPANY	
SHIPPING DATE	
TRACKING #	
ARRIVAL DATE	

ITEM #	DESCRIPTION	QTY	PRICE	FINAL PRICE

NOTES	
	SUBTOTAL	
	DISCOUNT	
	TAXES	
	SHIPPING	
	GRAND TOTAL	

ORDER FORM

ORDER #	
DATE	

CUSTOMER	
ADDRESS	
PHONE	
EMAIL	

STATUS	
O PAID / METHOD	
O SHIPPED	
O CANCELED	
EST. SHIPPING DATE	
SHIPPING COMPANY	
SHIPPING DATE	
TRACKING #	
ARRIVAL DATE	

ITEM #	DESCRIPTION	QTY	PRICE	FINAL PRICE

NOTES	SUBTOTAL	
	DISCOUNT	
	TAXES	
	SHIPPING	
	GRAND TOTAL	

ORDER FORM

ORDER #	
DATE	

CUSTOMER	
ADDRESS	
PHONE	
EMAIL	

STATUS

O PAID / METHOD

O SHIPPED

O CANCELED

EST. SHIPPING DATE	
SHIPPING COMPANY	
SHIPPING DATE	
TRACKING #	
ARRIVAL DATE	

ITEM #	DESCRIPTION	QTY	PRICE	FINAL PRICE

NOTES	SUBTOTAL	
	DISCOUNT	
	TAXES	
	SHIPPING	
	GRAND TOTAL	

ORDER FORM

ORDER #	
DATE	

CUSTOMER	
ADDRESS	
PHONE	
EMAIL	

STATUS	
O PAID / METHOD	
O SHIPPED	
O CANCELED	
EST. SHIPPING DATE	
SHIPPING COMPANY	
SHIPPING DATE	
TRACKING #	
ARRIVAL DATE	

ITEM #	DESCRIPTION	QTY	PRICE	FINAL PRICE

NOTES		SUBTOTAL	
		DISCOUNT	
		TAXES	
		SHIPPING	
		GRAND TOTAL	

ORDER FORM

ORDER #	
DATE	

CUSTOMER	
ADDRESS	
PHONE	
EMAIL	

STATUS	
O PAID / METHOD	
O SHIPPED	
O CANCELED	
EST. SHIPPING DATE	
SHIPPING COMPANY	
SHIPPING DATE	
TRACKING #	
ARRIVAL DATE	

ITEM #	DESCRIPTION	QTY	PRICE	FINAL PRICE

NOTES	SUBTOTAL	
	DISCOUNT	
	TAXES	
	SHIPPING	
	GRAND TOTAL	

ORDER FORM

ORDER #	
DATE	

CUSTOMER	
ADDRESS	
PHONE	
EMAIL	

STATUS	
O PAID / METHOD	
O SHIPPED	
O CANCELED	
EST. SHIPPING DATE	
SHIPPING COMPANY	
SHIPPING DATE	
TRACKING #	
ARRIVAL DATE	

ITEM #	DESCRIPTION	QTY	PRICE	FINAL PRICE

NOTES		
	SUBTOTAL	
	DISCOUNT	
	TAXES	
	SHIPPING	
	GRAND TOTAL	

ORDER FORM

ORDER #	
DATE	

CUSTOMER	
ADDRESS	
PHONE	
EMAIL	

STATUS	
O PAID / METHOD	
O SHIPPED	
O CANCELED	
EST. SHIPPING DATE	
SHIPPING COMPANY	
SHIPPING DATE	
TRACKING #	
ARRIVAL DATE	

ITEM #	DESCRIPTION	QTY	PRICE	FINAL PRICE

NOTES

SUBTOTAL	
DISCOUNT	
TAXES	
SHIPPING	
GRAND TOTAL	

ORDER FORM

ORDER #	
DATE	

CUSTOMER	
ADDRESS	
PHONE	
EMAIL	

STATUS	
O PAID / METHOD	
O SHIPPED	
O CANCELED	
EST. SHIPPING DATE	
SHIPPING COMPANY	
SHIPPING DATE	
TRACKING #	
ARRIVAL DATE	

ITEM #	DESCRIPTION	QTY	PRICE	FINAL PRICE

NOTES		SUBTOTAL	
		DISCOUNT	
		TAXES	
		SHIPPING	
		GRAND TOTAL	

ORDER FORM

ORDER #	.
DATE	

CUSTOMER	
ADDRESS	
PHONE	
EMAIL	

STATUS	
O PAID / METHOD	
O SHIPPED	
O CANCELED	
EST. SHIPPING DATE	
SHIPPING COMPANY	
SHIPPING DATE	
TRACKING #	
ARRIVAL DATE	

ITEM #	DESCRIPTION	QTY	PRICE	FINAL PRICE

NOTES

SUBTOTAL	
DISCOUNT	
TAXES	
SHIPPING	
GRAND TOTAL	

ORDER FORM

ORDER #	
DATE	

CUSTOMER	
ADDRESS	
PHONE	
EMAIL	

STATUS	
O PAID / METHOD	
O SHIPPED	
O CANCELED	
EST. SHIPPING DATE	
SHIPPING COMPANY	
SHIPPING DATE	
TRACKING #	
ARRIVAL DATE	

ITEM #	DESCRIPTION	QTY	PRICE	FINAL PRICE

NOTES		SUBTOTAL	
		DISCOUNT	
		TAXES	
		SHIPPING	
		GRAND TOTAL	

ORDER FORM

ORDER #	
DATE	

CUSTOMER	
ADDRESS	
PHONE	
EMAIL	

STATUS	
O PAID / METHOD	
O SHIPPED	
O CANCELED	
EST. SHIPPING DATE	
SHIPPING COMPANY	
SHIPPING DATE	
TRACKING #	
ARRIVAL DATE	

ITEM #	DESCRIPTION	QTY	PRICE	FINAL PRICE

NOTES		SUBTOTAL	
		DISCOUNT	
		TAXES	
		SHIPPING	
		GRAND TOTAL	

ORDER FORM

ORDER #	
DATE	

CUSTOMER	
ADDRESS	
PHONE	
EMAIL	

STATUS	
O PAID / METHOD	
O SHIPPED	
O CANCELED	
EST. SHIPPING DATE	
SHIPPING COMPANY	
SHIPPING DATE	
TRACKING #	
ARRIVAL DATE	

ITEM #	DESCRIPTION	QTY	PRICE	FINAL PRICE

NOTES

SUBTOTAL	
DISCOUNT	
TAXES	
SHIPPING	
GRAND TOTAL	

ORDER FORM

ORDER #	
DATE	

CUSTOMER	
ADDRESS	
PHONE	
EMAIL	

STATUS	
O PAID / METHOD	
O SHIPPED	
O CANCELED	
EST. SHIPPING DATE	
SHIPPING COMPANY	
SHIPPING DATE	
TRACKING #	
ARRIVAL DATE	

ITEM #	DESCRIPTION	QTY	PRICE	FINAL PRICE

NOTES	SUBTOTAL	
	DISCOUNT	
	TAXES	
	SHIPPING	
	GRAND TOTAL	

ORDER FORM

ORDER #	
DATE	

CUSTOMER	
ADDRESS	
PHONE	
EMAIL	

STATUS

O PAID / METHOD

O SHIPPED

O CANCELED

EST. SHIPPING DATE	
SHIPPING COMPANY	
SHIPPING DATE	
TRACKING #	
ARRIVAL DATE	

ITEM #	DESCRIPTION	QTY	PRICE	FINAL PRICE

NOTES

SUBTOTAL	
DISCOUNT	
TAXES	
SHIPPING	
GRAND TOTAL	

ORDER FORM

ORDER #	
DATE	

CUSTOMER	
ADDRESS	
PHONE	
EMAIL	

STATUS	
O PAID / METHOD	
O SHIPPED	
O CANCELED	
EST. SHIPPING DATE	
SHIPPING COMPANY	
SHIPPING DATE	
TRACKING #	
ARRIVAL DATE	

ITEM #	DESCRIPTION	QTY	PRICE	FINAL PRICE

NOTES		SUBTOTAL	
		DISCOUNT	
		TAXES	
		SHIPPING	
		GRAND TOTAL	

ORDER FORM

ORDER #	
DATE	

CUSTOMER	
ADDRESS	
PHONE	
EMAIL	

STATUS

O PAID / METHOD	
O SHIPPED	
O CANCELED	
EST. SHIPPING DATE	
SHIPPING COMPANY	
SHIPPING DATE	
TRACKING #	
ARRIVAL DATE	

ITEM #	DESCRIPTION	QTY	PRICE	FINAL PRICE

NOTES

SUBTOTAL	
DISCOUNT	
TAXES	
SHIPPING	
GRAND TOTAL	

ORDER FORM

ORDER #	
DATE	

CUSTOMER	
ADDRESS	
PHONE	
EMAIL	

STATUS	
O PAID / METHOD	
O SHIPPED	
O CANCELED	
EST. SHIPPING DATE	
SHIPPING COMPANY	
SHIPPING DATE	
TRACKING #	
ARRIVAL DATE	

ITEM #	DESCRIPTION	QTY	PRICE	FINAL PRICE

NOTES	SUBTOTAL	
	DISCOUNT	
	TAXES	
	SHIPPING	
	GRAND TOTAL	

ORDER FORM

ORDER #	
DATE	

CUSTOMER	
ADDRESS	
PHONE	
EMAIL	

STATUS	
O PAID / METHOD	
O SHIPPED	
O CANCELED	
EST. SHIPPING DATE	
SHIPPING COMPANY	
SHIPPING DATE	
TRACKING #	
ARRIVAL DATE	

ITEM #	DESCRIPTION	QTY	PRICE	FINAL PRICE

NOTES	SUBTOTAL	
	DISCOUNT	
	TAXES	
	SHIPPING	
	GRAND TOTAL	

ORDER FORM

ORDER #	
DATE	

CUSTOMER	
ADDRESS	
PHONE	
EMAIL	

STATUS	
O PAID / METHOD	
O SHIPPED	
O CANCELED	
EST. SHIPPING DATE	
SHIPPING COMPANY	
SHIPPING DATE	
TRACKING #	
ARRIVAL DATE	

ITEM #	DESCRIPTION	QTY	PRICE	FINAL PRICE

NOTES

SUBTOTAL	
DISCOUNT	
TAXES	
SHIPPING	
GRAND TOTAL	

ORDER FORM

ORDER #	
DATE	

CUSTOMER	
ADDRESS	
PHONE	
EMAIL	

STATUS	
O PAID / METHOD	
O SHIPPED	
O CANCELED	
EST. SHIPPING DATE	
SHIPPING COMPANY	
SHIPPING DATE	
TRACKING #	
ARRIVAL DATE	

ITEM #	DESCRIPTION	QTY	PRICE	FINAL PRICE

NOTES

SUBTOTAL	
DISCOUNT	
TAXES	
SHIPPING	
GRAND TOTAL	

ORDER FORM

ORDER #	
DATE	

CUSTOMER	
ADDRESS	
PHONE	
EMAIL	

STATUS	
O PAID / METHOD	
O SHIPPED	
O CANCELED	
EST. SHIPPING DATE	
SHIPPING COMPANY	
SHIPPING DATE	
TRACKING #	
ARRIVAL DATE	

ITEM #	DESCRIPTION	QTY	PRICE	FINAL PRICE

NOTES		SUBTOTAL	
		DISCOUNT	
		TAXES	
		SHIPPING	
		GRAND TOTAL	

ORDER FORM

ORDER #	
DATE	

CUSTOMER	
ADDRESS	
PHONE	
EMAIL	

STATUS	
O PAID / METHOD	
O SHIPPED	
O CANCELED	
EST. SHIPPING DATE	
SHIPPING COMPANY	
SHIPPING DATE	
TRACKING #	
ARRIVAL DATE	

ITEM #	DESCRIPTION	QTY	PRICE	FINAL PRICE

NOTES		SUBTOTAL	
		DISCOUNT	
		TAXES	
		SHIPPING	
		GRAND TOTAL	

ORDER FORM

ORDER #	
DATE	

CUSTOMER	
ADDRESS	
PHONE	
EMAIL	

STATUS	
O PAID / METHOD	
O SHIPPED	
O CANCELED	
EST. SHIPPING DATE	
SHIPPING COMPANY	
SHIPPING DATE	
TRACKING #	
ARRIVAL DATE	

ITEM #	DESCRIPTION	QTY	PRICE	FINAL PRICE

NOTES	SUBTOTAL	
	DISCOUNT	
	TAXES	
	SHIPPING	
	GRAND TOTAL	

ORDER FORM

ORDER #	
DATE	

CUSTOMER	
ADDRESS	
PHONE	
EMAIL	

STATUS	
O PAID / METHOD	
O SHIPPED	
O CANCELED	
EST. SHIPPING DATE	
SHIPPING COMPANY	
SHIPPING DATE	
TRACKING #	
ARRIVAL DATE	

ITEM #	DESCRIPTION	QTY	PRICE	FINAL PRICE

NOTES	SUBTOTAL	
	DISCOUNT	
	TAXES	
	SHIPPING	
	GRAND TOTAL	

ORDER FORM

ORDER #	
DATE	

CUSTOMER	
ADDRESS	
PHONE	
EMAIL	

STATUS	
O PAID / METHOD	
O SHIPPED	
O CANCELED	
EST. SHIPPING DATE	
SHIPPING COMPANY	
SHIPPING DATE	
TRACKING #	
ARRIVAL DATE	

ITEM #	DESCRIPTION	QTY	PRICE	FINAL PRICE

NOTES

SUBTOTAL	
DISCOUNT	
TAXES	
SHIPPING	
GRAND TOTAL	

ORDER FORM

ORDER #	
DATE	

CUSTOMER	
ADDRESS	
PHONE	
EMAIL	

STATUS

O PAID / METHOD

O SHIPPED

O CANCELED

EST. SHIPPING DATE	
SHIPPING COMPANY	
SHIPPING DATE	
TRACKING #	
ARRIVAL DATE	

ITEM #	DESCRIPTION	QTY	PRICE	FINAL PRICE

NOTES	SUBTOTAL	
	DISCOUNT	
	TAXES	
	SHIPPING	
	GRAND TOTAL	

ORDER FORM

ORDER #	
DATE	

CUSTOMER	
ADDRESS	
PHONE	
EMAIL	

STATUS

O PAID / METHOD

O SHIPPED

O CANCELED

EST. SHIPPING DATE	
SHIPPING COMPANY	
SHIPPING DATE	
TRACKING #	
ARRIVAL DATE	

ITEM #	DESCRIPTION	QTY	PRICE	FINAL PRICE

NOTES	SUBTOTAL	
	DISCOUNT	
	TAXES	
	SHIPPING	
	GRAND TOTAL	

ORDER FORM

ORDER #	
DATE	

CUSTOMER	
ADDRESS	
PHONE	
EMAIL	

STATUS	
O PAID / METHOD	
O SHIPPED	
O CANCELED	
EST. SHIPPING DATE	
SHIPPING COMPANY	
SHIPPING DATE	
TRACKING #	
ARRIVAL DATE	

ITEM #	DESCRIPTION	QTY	PRICE	FINAL PRICE

NOTES	SUBTOTAL	
	DISCOUNT	
	TAXES	
	SHIPPING	
	GRAND TOTAL	

ORDER FORM

ORDER #	
DATE	

CUSTOMER	
ADDRESS	
PHONE	
EMAIL	

STATUS	
O PAID / METHOD	
O SHIPPED	
O CANCELED	
EST. SHIPPING DATE	
SHIPPING COMPANY	
SHIPPING DATE	
TRACKING #	
ARRIVAL DATE	

ITEM #	DESCRIPTION	QTY	PRICE	FINAL PRICE

NOTES		SUBTOTAL	
		DISCOUNT	
		TAXES	
		SHIPPING	
		GRAND TOTAL	

ORDER FORM

ORDER #	
DATE	

CUSTOMER	
ADDRESS	
PHONE	
EMAIL	

STATUS	
O PAID / METHOD	
O SHIPPED	
O CANCELED	
EST. SHIPPING DATE	
SHIPPING COMPANY	
SHIPPING DATE	
TRACKING #	
ARRIVAL DATE	

ITEM #	DESCRIPTION	QTY	PRICE	FINAL PRICE

NOTES

SUBTOTAL	
DISCOUNT	
TAXES	
SHIPPING	
GRAND TOTAL	

ORDER FORM

ORDER #	
DATE	

CUSTOMER	
ADDRESS	
PHONE	
EMAIL	

STATUS	
O PAID / METHOD	
O SHIPPED	
O CANCELED	
EST. SHIPPING DATE	
SHIPPING COMPANY	
SHIPPING DATE	
TRACKING #	
ARRIVAL DATE	

ITEM #	DESCRIPTION	QTY	PRICE	FINAL PRICE

NOTES

SUBTOTAL	
DISCOUNT	
TAXES	
SHIPPING	
GRAND TOTAL	

ORDER FORM

ORDER #	
DATE	

CUSTOMER	
ADDRESS	
PHONE	
EMAIL	

STATUS	
O PAID / METHOD	
O SHIPPED	
O CANCELED	
EST. SHIPPING DATE	
SHIPPING COMPANY	
SHIPPING DATE	
TRACKING #	
ARRIVAL DATE	

ITEM #	DESCRIPTION	QTY	PRICE	FINAL PRICE

NOTES	SUBTOTAL	
	DISCOUNT	
	TAXES	
	SHIPPING	
	GRAND TOTAL	

ORDER FORM

ORDER #	
DATE	

CUSTOMER	
ADDRESS	
PHONE	
EMAIL	

STATUS	
O PAID / METHOD	
O SHIPPED	
O CANCELED	
EST. SHIPPING DATE	
SHIPPING COMPANY	
SHIPPING DATE	
TRACKING #	
ARRIVAL DATE	

ITEM #	DESCRIPTION	QTY	PRICE	FINAL PRICE

NOTES

SUBTOTAL	
DISCOUNT	
TAXES	
SHIPPING	
GRAND TOTAL	

ORDER FORM

ORDER #	
DATE	

STATUS	
O PAID / METHOD	
O SHIPPED	
O CANCELED	

CUSTOMER	
ADDRESS	
PHONE	
EMAIL	

EST. SHIPPING DATE	
SHIPPING COMPANY	
SHIPPING DATE	
TRACKING #	
ARRIVAL DATE	

ITEM #	DESCRIPTION	QTY	PRICE	FINAL PRICE

NOTES

SUBTOTAL	
DISCOUNT	
TAXES	
SHIPPING	
GRAND TOTAL	

ORDER FORM

ORDER #	
DATE	

CUSTOMER	
ADDRESS	
PHONE	
EMAIL	

STATUS	
O PAID / METHOD	
O SHIPPED	
O CANCELED	
EST. SHIPPING DATE	
SHIPPING COMPANY	
SHIPPING DATE	
TRACKING #	
ARRIVAL DATE	

ITEM #	DESCRIPTION	QTY	PRICE	FINAL PRICE

NOTES

SUBTOTAL	
DISCOUNT	
TAXES	
SHIPPING	
GRAND TOTAL	

ORDER FORM

ORDER #	
DATE	

CUSTOMER	
ADDRESS	
PHONE	
EMAIL	

STATUS	
O PAID / METHOD	
O SHIPPED	
O CANCELED	
EST. SHIPPING DATE	
SHIPPING COMPANY	
SHIPPING DATE	
TRACKING #	
ARRIVAL DATE	

ITEM #	DESCRIPTION	QTY	PRICE	FINAL PRICE

NOTES		SUBTOTAL	
		DISCOUNT	
		TAXES	
		SHIPPING	
		GRAND TOTAL	

ORDER FORM

ORDER #	
DATE	

CUSTOMER	
ADDRESS	
PHONE	
EMAIL	

STATUS	
O PAID / METHOD	
O SHIPPED	
O CANCELED	
EST. SHIPPING DATE	
SHIPPING COMPANY	
SHIPPING DATE	
TRACKING #	
ARRIVAL DATE	

ITEM #	DESCRIPTION	QTY	PRICE	FINAL PRICE

NOTES		SUBTOTAL	
		DISCOUNT	
		TAXES	
		SHIPPING	
		GRAND TOTAL	

ORDER FORM

ORDER #	
DATE	

CUSTOMER	
ADDRESS	
PHONE	
EMAIL	

STATUS	
○ PAID / METHOD	
○ SHIPPED	
○ CANCELED	
EST. SHIPPING DATE	
SHIPPING COMPANY	
SHIPPING DATE	
TRACKING #	
ARRIVAL DATE	

ITEM #	DESCRIPTION	QTY	PRICE	FINAL PRICE

NOTES

SUBTOTAL	
DISCOUNT	
TAXES	
SHIPPING	
GRAND TOTAL	

ORDER FORM

ORDER #	
DATE	

CUSTOMER	
ADDRESS	
PHONE	
EMAIL	

STATUS	
O PAID / METHOD	
O SHIPPED	
O CANCELED	
EST. SHIPPING DATE	
SHIPPING COMPANY	
SHIPPING DATE	
TRACKING #	
ARRIVAL DATE	

ITEM #	DESCRIPTION	QTY	PRICE	FINAL PRICE

NOTES	SUBTOTAL	
	DISCOUNT	
	TAXES	
	SHIPPING	
	GRAND TOTAL	

ORDER FORM

ORDER #	
DATE	

CUSTOMER	
ADDRESS	
PHONE	
EMAIL	

STATUS	
O PAID / METHOD	
O SHIPPED	
O CANCELED	
EST. SHIPPING DATE	
SHIPPING COMPANY	
SHIPPING DATE	
TRACKING #	
ARRIVAL DATE	

ITEM #	DESCRIPTION	QTY	PRICE	FINAL PRICE

NOTES

SUBTOTAL	
DISCOUNT	
TAXES	
SHIPPING	
GRAND TOTAL	

ORDER FORM

ORDER #	
DATE	

CUSTOMER	
ADDRESS	
PHONE	
EMAIL	

STATUS	
O PAID / METHOD	
O SHIPPED	
O CANCELED	
EST. SHIPPING DATE	
SHIPPING COMPANY	
SHIPPING DATE	
TRACKING #	
ARRIVAL DATE	

ITEM #	DESCRIPTION	QTY	PRICE	FINAL PRICE

NOTES	SUBTOTAL	
	DISCOUNT	
	TAXES	
	SHIPPING	
	GRAND TOTAL	

ORDER FORM

ORDER #	
DATE	

CUSTOMER	
ADDRESS	
PHONE	
EMAIL	

STATUS	
O PAID / METHOD	
O SHIPPED	
O CANCELED	
EST. SHIPPING DATE	
SHIPPING COMPANY	
SHIPPING DATE	
TRACKING #	
ARRIVAL DATE	

ITEM #	DESCRIPTION	QTY	PRICE	FINAL PRICE

NOTES	SUBTOTAL	
	DISCOUNT	
	TAXES	
	SHIPPING	
	GRAND TOTAL	

ORDER FORM

ORDER #	
DATE	

CUSTOMER	
ADDRESS	
PHONE	
EMAIL	

STATUS	
O PAID / METHOD	
O SHIPPED	
O CANCELED	
EST. SHIPPING DATE	
SHIPPING COMPANY	
SHIPPING DATE	
TRACKING #	
ARRIVAL DATE	

ITEM #	DESCRIPTION	QTY	PRICE	FINAL PRICE

NOTES

SUBTOTAL	
DISCOUNT	
TAXES	
SHIPPING	
GRAND TOTAL	

ORDER FORM

ORDER #	
DATE	

CUSTOMER	
ADDRESS	
PHONE	
EMAIL	

STATUS	
O PAID / METHOD	
O SHIPPED	
O CANCELED	
EST. SHIPPING DATE	
SHIPPING COMPANY	
SHIPPING DATE	
TRACKING #	
ARRIVAL DATE	

ITEM #	DESCRIPTION	QTY	PRICE	FINAL PRICE

NOTES

SUBTOTAL	
DISCOUNT	
TAXES	
SHIPPING	
GRAND TOTAL	

ORDER FORM

ORDER #	
DATE	

CUSTOMER	
ADDRESS	
PHONE	
EMAIL	

STATUS	
O PAID / METHOD	
O SHIPPED	
O CANCELED	
EST. SHIPPING DATE	
SHIPPING COMPANY	
SHIPPING DATE	
TRACKING #	
ARRIVAL DATE	

ITEM #	DESCRIPTION	QTY	PRICE	FINAL PRICE

NOTES

SUBTOTAL	
DISCOUNT	
TAXES	
SHIPPING	
GRAND TOTAL	

ORDER FORM

ORDER #	
DATE	

CUSTOMER	
ADDRESS	
PHONE	
EMAIL	

STATUS	
O PAID / METHOD	
O SHIPPED	
O CANCELED	
EST. SHIPPING DATE	
SHIPPING COMPANY	
SHIPPING DATE	
TRACKING #	
ARRIVAL DATE	

ITEM #	DESCRIPTION	QTY	PRICE	FINAL PRICE

NOTES	SUBTOTAL	
	DISCOUNT	
	TAXES	
	SHIPPING	
	GRAND TOTAL	

ORDER FORM

ORDER #	
DATE	

CUSTOMER	
ADDRESS	
PHONE	
EMAIL	

STATUS	
O PAID / METHOD	
O SHIPPED	
O CANCELED	
EST. SHIPPING DATE	
SHIPPING COMPANY	
SHIPPING DATE	
TRACKING #	
ARRIVAL DATE	

ITEM #	DESCRIPTION	QTY	PRICE	FINAL PRICE

NOTES

SUBTOTAL	
DISCOUNT	
TAXES	
SHIPPING	
GRAND TOTAL	

ORDER FORM

ORDER #	
DATE	

CUSTOMER	
ADDRESS	
PHONE	
EMAIL	

STATUS

O PAID / METHOD

O SHIPPED

O CANCELED

EST. SHIPPING DATE	
SHIPPING COMPANY	
SHIPPING DATE	
TRACKING #	
ARRIVAL DATE	

ITEM #	DESCRIPTION	QTY	PRICE	FINAL PRICE

NOTES

SUBTOTAL	
DISCOUNT	
TAXES	
SHIPPING	
GRAND TOTAL	

ORDER FORM

ORDER #	
DATE	

CUSTOMER	
ADDRESS	
PHONE	
EMAIL	

STATUS

- ○ PAID / METHOD
- ○ SHIPPED
- ○ CANCELED

EST. SHIPPING DATE	
SHIPPING COMPANY	
SHIPPING DATE	
TRACKING #	
ARRIVAL DATE	

ITEM #	DESCRIPTION	QTY	PRICE	FINAL PRICE

NOTES

SUBTOTAL	
DISCOUNT	
TAXES	
SHIPPING	
GRAND TOTAL	

ORDER FORM

ORDER #	
DATE	

CUSTOMER	
ADDRESS	
PHONE	
EMAIL	

STATUS	
O PAID / METHOD	
O SHIPPED	
O CANCELED	
EST. SHIPPING DATE	
SHIPPING COMPANY	
SHIPPING DATE	
TRACKING #	
ARRIVAL DATE	

ITEM #	DESCRIPTION	QTY	PRICE	FINAL PRICE

NOTES

SUBTOTAL	
DISCOUNT	
TAXES	
SHIPPING	
GRAND TOTAL	

ORDER FORM

ORDER #	
DATE	

CUSTOMER	
ADDRESS	
PHONE	
EMAIL	

STATUS	
O PAID / METHOD	
O SHIPPED	
O CANCELED	
EST. SHIPPING DATE	
SHIPPING COMPANY	
SHIPPING DATE	
TRACKING #	
ARRIVAL DATE	

ITEM #	DESCRIPTION	QTY	PRICE	FINAL PRICE

NOTES

SUBTOTAL	
DISCOUNT	
TAXES	
SHIPPING	
GRAND TOTAL	

ORDER FORM

ORDER #	
DATE	

CUSTOMER	
ADDRESS	
PHONE	
EMAIL	

STATUS	
O PAID / METHOD	
O SHIPPED	
O CANCELED	
EST. SHIPPING DATE	
SHIPPING COMPANY	
SHIPPING DATE	
TRACKING #	
ARRIVAL DATE	

ITEM #	DESCRIPTION	QTY	PRICE	FINAL PRICE

NOTES

SUBTOTAL	
DISCOUNT	
TAXES	
SHIPPING	
GRAND TOTAL	

ORDER FORM

ORDER #	
DATE	

CUSTOMER	
ADDRESS	
PHONE	
EMAIL	

STATUS	
O PAID / METHOD	
O SHIPPED	
O CANCELED	
EST. SHIPPING DATE	
SHIPPING COMPANY	
SHIPPING DATE	
TRACKING #	
ARRIVAL DATE	

ITEM #	DESCRIPTION	QTY	PRICE	FINAL PRICE

NOTES

SUBTOTAL	
DISCOUNT	
TAXES	
SHIPPING	
GRAND TOTAL	

ORDER FORM

ORDER #	
DATE	

CUSTOMER	
ADDRESS	
PHONE	
EMAIL	

STATUS	
O PAID / METHOD	
O SHIPPED	
O CANCELED	
EST. SHIPPING DATE	
SHIPPING COMPANY	
SHIPPING DATE	
TRACKING #	
ARRIVAL DATE	

ITEM #	DESCRIPTION	QTY	PRICE	FINAL PRICE

NOTES	

SUBTOTAL	
DISCOUNT	
TAXES	
SHIPPING	
GRAND TOTAL	

ORDER FORM

ORDER #	
DATE	

CUSTOMER	
ADDRESS	
PHONE	
EMAIL	

STATUS	
O PAID / METHOD	
O SHIPPED	
O CANCELED	
EST. SHIPPING DATE	
SHIPPING COMPANY	
SHIPPING DATE	
TRACKING #	
ARRIVAL DATE	

ITEM #	DESCRIPTION	QTY	PRICE	FINAL PRICE

NOTES

SUBTOTAL	
DISCOUNT	
TAXES	
SHIPPING	
GRAND TOTAL	

www.ingramcontent.com/pod-product-compliance
Lightning Source LLC
Chambersburg PA
CBHW051757200326
41597CB00025B/4588